P9-DJK-863

ONE
WITH
CHRIST

ONE
WITH
CHRIST

HUDSON
TAYLOR

Whitaker House

Unless otherwise indicated, all Scripture quotations are taken from the *King James Version* (KJV) of the Bible.

Scripture quotations marked (RV) are taken from the *Revised Version* of the Holy Bible.

ONE WITH CHRIST

ISBN: 0-88368-061-0
Printed in the United States of America
Copyright © 1997 by Whitaker House

Whitaker House
30 Hunt Valley Circle
New Kensington, PA 15068

2 3 4 5 6 7 8 9 10 11 12 13 / 06 05 04 03 02 01 00 99

Contents

Chapter 1

No Better Song!

The song of songs, which is Solomon's.
—Song of Solomon 1:1

This book is well called *the* song of songs! There is no song like it. If it is read properly, it brings a gladness to the heart that is as far beyond the joy of earthly things as heaven is higher than the earth. It has been well said that this is a song that grace alone can teach, and experience alone can learn.

Our Savior, speaking of the union of the branch with the vine, said, *"These things have I spoken unto you, that my joy might remain in you, and that your joy might be full"* (John 15:11). And the Beloved Disciple, writing of Him who *"was from the beginning,"* who *"was with the Father, and was manifested unto us"* (1 John 1:1–2) in order that we might share the fellowship that He enjoyed, also said,

"These things write we unto you, that your joy may be full" (1 John 1:4).

Union with Christ and abiding in Christ: what don't they secure? Peace, perfect peace; rest, constant rest; answers to all our prayers; victory over all our foes; pure, holy living; ever increasing fruitfulness—all of these are the glad outcome of abiding in Christ. The practical use of the Song of Solomon is to deepen this union and to make this abiding in Christ more constant.

THE NEW TESTAMENT CONNECTION

"All scripture is given by inspiration of God, and is profitable" (2 Tim. 3:16), and therefore no part is, or can be, neglected without loss. Our purpose in studying God's inspired Word is that we may know *"that God may be all in all"* (1 Cor. 15:28). Christ's teaching in John 17:3, *"And this is* [the object of] *life eternal, that they might know thee the only true God, and Jesus Christ, whom thou hast sent,"* agrees with this. Should we not then act wisely by keeping this object always in view in our daily life and study of God's holy Word?

Few portions of Scripture will help the devout believer more in the pursuit of this all-important knowledge of God than the too-much neglected Song of Solomon. Like other portions of the Bible, this book has its difficulties. But so have all the works of God. Is not the fact that they surpass our unaided powers of comprehension and research an indicator of divinity? Can man, whose mind is finite, expect to grasp infinite divine power or to understand and interpret the works or the providence of the all-wise God? And if not, is it surprising that His Word also needs superhuman wisdom for its interpretation? Thanks be to God that the illumination of the Holy Spirit is promised to all who seek it. What more can we desire?

The key to the Song of Solomon is easily found in the teachings of the New Testament. Read without this key, the book is especially unintelligible. The Incarnate Word is the true key to the written Word. But even before the Incarnation, the devout student of the Old Testament could find much help for understanding the sacred mysteries of this book in the prophetic writings, for there Israel was taught that her Maker was her Husband (Isa. 54:5). John the Baptist, the last of the prophets, recognized the Bridegroom in the person of Christ and said,

> *He that hath the bride is the bridegroom: but the friend of the bridegroom,*

*which standeth and heareth him, re-
joiceth greatly because of the bridegroom's voice: this my joy therefore is
fulfilled.* (John 3:29)

Paul, in the fifth chapter of the epistle to
the Ephesians, went still further and taught
that the union of Christ with His church, and
her subjection to Him, underlies the very relationship of marriage and affords the pattern
for every godly union.

In Solomon, who is the bridegroom-king as
well as the author of this poem, we have a rep-
resentation of our Lord, the true Prince of
Peace, in His coming reign on earth. When this
occurs in actuality, not only will there be His
bride, the church, but also a willing people, His
subjects, over whom He will reign gloriously.
Then distant sovereigns will bring their wealth
and will behold the glory of the enthroned
King, proving Him with hard questions, as the
queen of Sheba once did to King Solomon.

They to whom this privilege is accorded will
be blessed. A brief glance will be enough for
them for a lifetime, but what will be the royal
dignity and blessedness of the risen and exalted
bride! Forever with her Lord, forever like her
Lord, forever conscious that His desire is toward
her, she will share His heart and His throne

alike. Can a study of the book that helps us to understand these mysteries of grace and love be anything other than most profitable?

It is interesting to notice the contrast between this book and the one preceding it. The book of Ecclesiastes teaches emphatically that *"vanity of vanities; all is vanity"* (Eccl. 1:2), and thus this book is the necessary introduction to the Song of Solomon, which shows how true blessing and satisfaction are to be possessed.

In the same way, our Savior's teaching in the fourth chapter of John points out the powerlessness of earthly things to give lasting satisfaction. This is in striking contrast to the flow of blessing that results from the presence of the Holy Spirit, whose work it is to reveal not Himself but Christ as the Bridegroom of the soul:

> *Whosoever drinketh of this water shall thirst again: but whosoever drinketh of the water that I shall give him shall never thirst; but the water that I shall give him shall be in him a well of water springing up* [overflowing, on and on] *into everlasting life.*   *(John 4:13–14)*

STUDYING THE SONG OF SOLOMON

Throughout this book of the Bible, we will find the speakers to be the following: the bride, the Bridegroom, and the daughters of Jerusalem. It is not usually difficult to ascertain the speaker, though people have come to different conclusions regarding some of the verses. The bride speaks of the Bridegroom as her "Beloved," the Bridegroom speaks of her as His "love," while the addresses of the daughters of Jerusalem are more varied. They vary among "the fairest among women"; "the Shulamite," or the King's bride; and also the "Prince's daughter."

Throughout this study of the Song of Solomon, it will be helpful to break up the book into six sections. The chapters that follow will deal with each of these sections. It will be observed that the bride is the chief speaker in sections one (Song 1:2–2:7) and two (Song 2:8–3:5), sections in which she is much occupied with herself. But in section three (Song 3:6–5:1), where the communion with the Bridegroom is unbroken, she has little to say and appears as the hearer. Also in this section, the daughters of Jerusalem give a long address, and the Bridegroom has His longest. He calls the betrothed His bride for the first time and calls her to fellowship in service.

In section four (Song 5:2–6:10), the bride again is the chief speaker, but after her restoration, the Bridegroom speaks at length and *"upbraideth not"* (James 1:5). In section five (Song 6:11–8:4), the bride is no longer called "the fairest among women," but she claims herself to be, and is recognized as, the royal bride. In section six (Song 8:5–14), the Bridegroom claims her from her very birth, and not merely from her betrothal, as God claimed Israel in Ezekiel 16.

> In the secret of His presence
>   How my soul delights to hide!
> Oh, how precious are the lessons
>   Which I learn at Jesus' side!
> Earthly cares can never vex me,
>   Neither trials lay me low;
> For when Satan comes to vex me,
>   To the secret place I go!

Chapter 2

The Unsatisfied Life and Its Remedy

Song of Solomon 1:2–2:7

There is no difficulty in recognizing the bride as the speaker in verses two through seven in this first section of the Song of Solomon. The words are not those of one dead in trespasses and sins, to whom the Lord is as a root out of a dry ground, without form and beauty (Isa. 53:2). The speaker has had her eyes opened to behold the Lord's beauty and longs for a fuller enjoyment of His love: *"Let him kiss me with the kisses of his mouth: for thy love is better than wine"* (Song 1:2).

It is good that it is so. It marks a distinct stage in the development of the life of grace in the soul. And this recorded experience gives us a divine warrant for the desire for perceptible manifestations of the Lord's presence and perceptible communications of His love. It was not always so with the bride. Once she was contented in His absence; other society and other occupations took up her interest. But now it can never be so again. The world can never be to her what it once was. The betrothed bride has learned to love her Lord, and no other society than His can satisfy her.

His visits may be occasional and may be brief, but they are precious times of enjoyment. Their memory is cherished in the intervals, and their repetition is longed for. There is no real satisfaction in His absence, and yet, alas, He is not always with her. He comes and goes. Now her joy in Him is a heaven below, but again she is longing, and longing in vain, for His presence. Like the ever changing tide, her experience is an ebbing and flowing one. It may even be that unrest is the rule, and satisfaction the exception. Is there no help for this? Must it always continue so? Has He, can He have, created these unquenchable longings only to tantalize them?

It would be strange indeed if this were the case. Yet are there not many of the Lord's people whose habitual experience corresponds with the bride's? They do not know the rest and the joy of abiding in Christ, and they do not know how to attain it or why it is not theirs. Are there not many who look back to the delightful times of their first betrothals, who, far from finding richer inheritance in Christ than they then had, are conscious that they have lost their first love (Rev. 2:4)? Might they express their experience in the sad lament:

> Where is the blessedness I knew
> When first I saw the Lord?

Again, others, who may not have lost their first love, may yet be feeling that the occasional interruptions to communion are becoming more and more unbearable as the world becomes less and He becomes more. His absence is an ever increasing distress. *"Oh that I knew where I might find him!"* (Job 23:3). *"Let him kiss me with the kisses of his mouth: for thy love is better than wine"* (Song 1:2). One may say, "If only His love were strong and constant like mine and He never withdrew the light of His countenance!"

Poor mistaken one! There is a love that is far stronger than your waiting, and it is longing for satisfaction. The Bridegroom is waiting for you all the time. The conditions that preclude His approach are all of your own making. Take the right place before Him, and He will be most ready, most glad, to satisfy your deepest longings and to meet and supply your every need.

What would we think of a betrothed one whose conceit and self-will prevented not only the consummation of her own joy, but of the one who had given her his heart? Never at rest in his absence, she cannot trust him fully, and she does not care to give up her own name, her own rights and possessions, and her own will to him who has become necessary for her happiness. She would gladly claim him fully without giving herself fully to him, but it can never be. While she retains her own name, she can never claim his. She cannot promise to love and honor if she will not also promise to obey, and until her love reaches that point of surrender, she must remain an unsatisfied lover. She cannot find rest as a satisfied bride in the home of her husband. While she retains her own will, and the control of her own possessions, she must be content to live on her own resources. She cannot claim his.

Could there be a sadder proof of the extent and reality of the Fall than the deep-seated distrust of our loving Lord and Master that makes us hesitate to give ourselves entirely up to Him? This distrust also makes us fear that He might require something beyond our powers or call for something that we would find it hard to give or to do.

The real secret of an unsatisfied life lies too often in an unsurrendered will. And yet how foolish, as well as how wrong, this is! Do we imagine that we are wiser than He or that our love for ourselves is stronger and tenderer than His? Do we think that we know ourselves better than He does? How our distrust must grieve and wound afresh the tender heart of Him who was for us the Man of Sorrows! What would be the feelings of an earthly bridegroom if he discovered that his fiancée was dreading the thought of marrying him, for fear that when he had the power, he would render her life unbearable? Yet how many of the Lord's redeemed ones treat Him just so! No wonder they are neither happy nor satisfied!

SURRENDERING TO LOVE

True love cannot be stationary; it must either decline or grow. Despite all the unworthy fears of our poor hearts, divine love is destined to conquer. The bride exclaims, *"Because of the savour of thy good ointments thy name is as ointment poured forth, therefore do the virgins love thee"* (Song 1:3). There was no better ointment than that with which the High Priest was anointed. Our Bridegroom is a Priest as well as a King. The trembling bride cannot wholly dismiss her fears, but the unrest and the longing become unbearable. She then determines to surrender all and let what fully follows come as it may. She will yield her very self to Him: heart and hand, influence and possessions. Nothing can be so intolerable as His absence! If He goes to another Moriah (Gen. 22:2), or even to a Calvary, she will follow Him: *"Draw me, we will run after thee"* (v. 4).

But, what follows is a wondrously glad surprise. No Moriah, no Calvary; on the contrary, a King! When the heart submits, then Jesus reigns. And when Jesus reigns, there is rest.

And where does He lead His bride? *"The king hath brought me into his chambers"* (v. 4). Not first to the banqueting house—that will come in due season—but first to be alone with Him.

How perfect! Could we be satisfied to meet a loved one only in public? No; we want to take such a one aside to have him all to ourselves. It is the same with our Master. He takes His now fully consecrated bride aside to taste and enjoy the sacred intimacies of His wondrous love. The Bridegroom of the church longs for communion with His people more than they long for fellowship with Him, and often He has to cry, *"Let me see thy countenance, let me hear thy voice; for sweet is thy voice, and thy countenance is comely"* (Song 2:14).

Are we not all too apt to seek Him for our needs instead of for His joy and pleasure? This should not be. We do not admire selfish children who only think of what they can get from their parents and are unmindful of the pleasure that they may give or the service that they may render. But, are we not in danger of forgetting that pleasing God means giving Him pleasure? Some of us look back to the time when the words "to please God" meant no more than not to sin against Him, not to grieve Him. But, would the love of earthly parents be satisfied with the mere absence of disobedience? Or would a bridegroom be satisfied if his bride only sought him for the supply of her own needs?

A word about morning devotions may not be out of place here. There is no time so profitably spent as the early hour that is given only to Jesus. Do we give sufficient attention to this hour? If possible, it should be redeemed; nothing can make up for it. We must take time to be holy! One other thought: When we bring our questions to God, do we not sometimes either go on to offer some other petition or leave our prayer time without waiting for replies? Does this not seem to show little expectation of an answer, and little desire for one? Is that the way we would like to be treated? Quiet waiting before God would save many from mistakes and many from sorrows.

We have found the bride making a glad discovery of a King—her King—and not a cross as she expected. This is the first result of her consecration. *"We will be glad and rejoice in thee, we will remember thy love more than wine: the upright love thee"* (Song 1:4).

Another discovery that is not any less important awaits her. She has seen the face of the King, and as the rising sun reveals what was hidden in the darkness so His light has revealed her blackness to her. She cries, *"I am black."* *"But comely"* (Song 1:5), interjects the Bridegroom with inimitable grace and tenderness. "No, I am black *'as the tents of Kedar'* (v. 5)," she continues. "Yet to Me," He responds, "you are *'comely...as the curtains of Solomon'* (v. 5)."

Nothing humbles the soul like sacred and intimate communion with the Lord, yet there is a sweet joy in feeling that He knows all and, notwithstanding, loves us still. Things once called "little negligences" are seen with new eyes in the secret of His presence. There we see the mistake, the sin, of not keeping our own vineyard. The bride confesses this:

Look not upon me, because I am black,
because the sun hath looked upon me:

> *my mother's children were angry with*
> *me; they made me the keeper of the vine-*
> *yards; but mine own vineyard have I not*
> *kept.* (Song 1:6)

Our attention is drawn here to a danger that is preeminently one of our day: the intense activity of our times may lead to zeal in service to the neglect of personal communion. However, such neglect will not only lessen the value of the service, but will tend to incapacitate us for the highest service. If we are watchful over the souls of others but neglect our own—if we are seeking to remove the speck from our brother's eye, unmindful of the beam in our own—we will often be disappointed with our powerlessness to help others, while our Master will be more disappointed in us.

Let us never forget that what we are is more important than what we do, and that all fruit borne when not abiding in Christ must be fruit of the flesh and not of the Spirit. The sin of neglected communion may be forgiven, and yet the effect may remain permanently, as wounds often leave a scar behind once they have healed.

UNION WITH THE BRIDEGROOM

We now come to a very sweet evidence of the reality of the heart-union of the bride with her Lord. She is one with the Good Shepherd. Her heart immediately and instinctively goes forth to the feeding of the flock, but she will tread in the footsteps of Him whom her soul loves, and she will not labor alone, or in companionship other than His own.

> *Tell me, O thou whom my soul loveth,*
> *where thou feedest, where thou makest*
> *thy flock to rest at noon: for why should*
> *I be as one that turneth aside by the*
> *flocks of thy companions?*   *(Song 1:7)*

She will not mistake the society of His servants for that of their Master.

> *If thou know not, O thou fairest among*
> *women, go thy way forth by the footsteps*
> *of the flock, and feed thy kids beside the*
> *shepherds' tents.*   *(v. 8)*

The above words are spoken by the daughters of Jerusalem and give a correct reply to the bride's questionings. If she shows her love to her Lord by feeding His sheep and by caring for His lambs (John 21:15–17), she need not fear to miss His presence. While sharing with others who are under the Shepherd in caring for His flock, she will find the Chief Shepherd at her side and will enjoy the signs of His approval. It will be service with Jesus as well as for Jesus.

But far sweeter than the reply of the daughters of Jerusalem is the voice of the Bridegroom, who now speaks Himself. It is the living fruit of her heart-oneness with Him that makes His love break forth in the joyful utterances of verses nine through eleven in chapter one. It is true that our love for our Lord will show itself in feeding His sheep. However, it is also true that He who once said, *"Inasmuch as ye have done it unto one of the least of these my brethren, ye have done it unto me"* (Matt. 25:40), has His own heart stirred and frequently reveals Himself in a special way to those who are ministering for Him.

The commendation of the bride in verse nine is one of striking appropriateness and beauty: *"I have compared thee, O my love, to a company of horses in Pharaoh's chariots."* It will be remembered that horses originally came out of Egypt and that the pure breed still found in Arabia during Solomon's reign was brought by his merchants to all the kings of the East. Those selected for Pharaoh's own chariot would not only be of the purest blood and perfect in proportion and symmetry, but also perfect in training, docile, and obedient. They would know no will but that of the charioteer, and the only object of their existence would be to carry the king wherever he wanted to go.

It should be so with the church of Christ: one body with many members, indwelt and guided by one Spirit; supporting the Head, and knowing no will but His. The church's rapid and harmonious movement should cause His kingdom to progress throughout the world.

Many years ago, a beloved friend, returning from the East by the overland route, made the journey from Suez to Cairo in a stagecoach. Upon boarding the coach, the passengers took their places, and about a dozen wild young horses were harnessed with ropes to the vehicle. The driver took his seat and cracked his whip, and the horses dashed off. Some went to the right, some went to the left, and others forward. This caused the coach to start with a jolt, and as suddenly to stop, with the effect of first throwing those sitting in the front seat into the laps of those sitting behind, and then of reversing the operation. With the aid of a sufficient number of Arabs, who ran on each side to keep these wild animals progressing in the right direction, the passengers were jerked and jolted, bruised and shaken, until, on reaching their destination, they were too wearied and sore to take the rest they so much needed.

Is the church of God today not more like these untrained steeds than a company of horses used for Pharaoh's chariot? And while self-will and disunion are apparent in the church, can we wonder that the *"world lieth in wickedness"* (1 John 5:19) and that heathen nations are barely touched by the Gospel?

Changing His simile, the Bridegroom continues: *"Thy cheeks are comely with rows of jewels, thy neck with chains of gold. We will make thee borders of gold with studs of silver"* (Song 1:10–11). The bride is not only beautiful and useful to her Lord, but she is also adorned, and it is His delight to add to her adornments. And His gifts are not perishable flowers or trinkets destitute of intrinsic value. The finest of gold, the purest of silver, and the most precious and lasting of jewels are the gifts of the Royal Bridegroom to His spouse. These, braided into her own hair, increase the pleasure of Him who has bestowed them.

In verses twelve through fourteen the bride responds: *"While the king sitteth at his table, my spikenard sendeth forth the smell thereof"* (v. 12). It is in His presence and through His grace that whatever fragrance or beauty that may be found in us comes forth. All that is gracious and divine is of Him as its source, through Him as its instrument, and to

Him as its end. But He Himself is far better than all His grace that works in us.

> *A bundle of myrrh is my wellbeloved unto me; he shall lie all night betwixt my breasts. My beloved is unto me as a cluster of camphire in the vineyards of Engedi.* (vv. 13–14)

It is good when our eyes are filled with His beauty and our hearts are occupied with Him. In the measure in which this is true of us we will recognize the correlative truth that His great heart is occupied with us. Note the response of the Bridegroom: *"Behold, thou art fair, my love; behold, thou art fair; thou hast doves' eyes"* (Song 1:15). How can the Bridegroom truthfully use such words of one who recognizes herself as *"black...as the tents of Kedar"* (v. 5)? And still stronger are the Bridegroom's words in Song of Solomon 4:7: *"Thou art all fair, my love; there is no spot in thee."*

We will find the solution to this difficulty in 2 Corinthians 3. Moses, in contemplation of the divine glory, became so transformed that the Israelites were not able to look on the glory of his countenance (v.7). In the same way,

> *We all, with open face beholding as in a glass the glory of the Lord, are changed*

into the same image from glory to glory
[i.e., the brightness caught from His
glory transforms us to glory], *even as by
the Spirit of the Lord.*   (v. 18)

Every mirror has two surfaces. The one is
dull and unreflecting and is all spots. But when
the reflecting surface is turned toward us, we
see no spots—we see our own image. So while
the bride is delighting in the beauty of the
Bridegroom, He beholds His own image in her.
There is no spot in that; it is all fair. May we
always present this reflection to His gaze and
to the world in which we live for the very purpose of reflecting Him.

Note again His words, *"thou hast doves'
eyes"* (Song 1:15). The hawk is a beautiful bird
and has beautiful eyes, quick and penetrating,
but the Bridegroom does not desire hawks'
eyes in His bride. The tender eyes of the inno-
cent dove are those that He admires. It was as
a dove that the Holy Spirit came upon Him at
His baptism, and a dovelike character is what
He seeks in each of His people.

The reason why David was not permitted
to build the temple was a very significant one.
His life was far from perfect, and his mistakes
and sins have been faithfully recorded by the
Holy Spirit. They brought upon him God's

chastening, yet it was not any of these that disqualified him from building the temple, but rather his warlike spirit. This was so despite the fact that many of his battles, if not all, were for the establishment of God's kingdom and the fulfillment of His promises to Abraham, Isaac, and Jacob.

Only Solomon, the prince of peace, could build the temple. If we want to be soulwinners and build up the church, which is His temple, let us note this: not by discussion or by argument, but by lifting up Christ will we draw men to Him.

ABIDING IN HIS LOVE

We now come to the reply of the bride. He has called her fair. She well replies wisely,

Behold thou art fair, my beloved, yea, pleasant: also our bed is green. The beams of our house are cedar, and our rafters of fir. I am [but a] rose of Sharon, and the lily of the valleys. (Song 1:16–2:1)

The last words are often quoted as though they were the utterance of the Bridegroom, but I believe they are called so incorrectly. The bride says, in effect, "You called me fair and pleasant; the fairness and pleasantness are Yours. I am but a wildflower, a lowly, scentless rose of Sharon [i.e., the autumn crocus] or a lily of the valley."

To this the Bridegroom responds: "Be it so. But if a wildflower, yet *'as the lily among thorns, so is my love among the daughters'* (Song 2:2)." And again the bride replies:

> *As the apple tree among the trees of the wood, so is my beloved among the sons. I sat down under his shadow with great delight, and his fruit was sweet to my taste.* (v. 3)

The apple tree is a beautiful tree, affording delightful shade as well as refreshing fruit. A humble wildflower herself, the bride recognizes her Bridegroom as a noble tree, both ornamental and fruitful. She finds in Him shade from the burning sun, refreshment, and rest. What a contrast between her present position and feelings and those with which this section commenced! The Bridegroom knew full well the cause of all her fears; her distrust sprang from her ignorance of Him. So He took her aside, and in the sweet intimacies of mutual love, her fears and distrust have vanished like the mists of the morning before the rising sun.

But now that she has learned to know Him, she has a further experience of His love. He is not ashamed to acknowledge her publicly: *"He brought me to the banqueting house, and his banner over me was love"* (Song 2:4).

A public place is now as appropriate as the King's chambers were. Fearlessly and without shame, she can sit at His side as His acknowledged spouse, the bride of His choice. Overwhelmed with His love, she exclaims,

> *Stay me with flagons, comfort me with apples: for I am sick of love. His left hand is under my head, and his right hand doth embrace me.*　　*(vv. 5–6)*

Now she finds the blessedness of being possessed. Since she is no longer her own, heart-rest is both her right and her enjoyment, and this is how the Bridegroom would have it.

> *I charge you, O ye daughters of Jerusalem, by the roes, and by the hinds of the field, that ye stir not up, nor awake my love, till* [she] *please.*　　*(Song 2:7)*

The pronoun at the end of this verse, which is also in 3:5 and 8:4, should not be "he" as it is in the King James Version or "it" as it is in the Revised Version, but rather "she."

It is never His will that our rest in Him be disturbed.

> You may always be abiding,
>   If you will, at Jesus' side;
> In the secret of His presence
>   You may every moment hide.

There is no change in His love. He is the same yesterday, today, and forever (Heb. 13:8). To us, He promises, *"I will never leave thee, nor forsake thee"* (v. 5), and His earnest exhortation and command is, *"'Abide in me,'* and I will abide in you" (John 15:4).

Chapter 3

Communion Broken and Restored

Song of Solomon 2:8–3:5

At the close of the first section of the Song of Solomon, we left the bride satisfied and at rest in the arms of her Beloved, who had charged the daughters of Jerusalem not to stir up or awaken His love until she wanted to be awakened. We might suppose that a union so complete, a satisfaction so full, would never be interrupted by failure on the part of the happy bride.

Unfortunately, the experience of most of us shows how easily communion with Christ may be broken. The exhortations of our Lord to those who are indeed branches of the true Vine (John 15:1) and cleansed by the word that He has spoken (v.3) are quite needful in order for them to abide in Him (v. 4). The failure is never on His side. *"Lo, I am with you alway"*

33

(Matt. 28:20). But, the bride often forgets the exhortation that can be found in Psalm 45:

> *Hearken, O daughter, and consider, and incline thine ear; forget also thine own people, and thy father's house; so shall the King greatly desire thy beauty: for he is thy Lord; and worship thou him.*
>
> *(vv. 10–11)*

FALLING AWAY

> *Therefore we ought to give the more earnest heed to the things that were heard, lest haply we drift away from them.*
>
> *(Hebrews 2:1 RV)*

In this section the bride has drifted back from her position of blessing into a state of worldliness. Perhaps the very restfulness of her newfound joy made her feel too secure. Perhaps she thought that, as far as she was concerned, there was no need for the exhortation, *"Keep yourselves from idols"* (1 John 5:21). Or she may have thought that her love of the world was so thoroughly taken away that she might safely go back, and, by a little compromise on her part, might win her friends to her Lord, too.

Maybe she scarcely thought at all. Since she was glad that she was saved and free, she may have forgotten that the current—the course of this world—was against her. She unknowingly drifted back to that position out of which she was called, unaware all the time of backsliding. It is not necessary, when the current is against us, to turn the boat's bow downstream in order to drift, or for a runner in a race to turn back in order to miss the prize.

Ah, how often the Enemy succeeds, by one device or another, in tempting the believer away from that position of entire consecration to Christ in which alone the fullness of His power and of His love can be experienced. We say the fullness of His power and of His love, for the believer may not have ceased to love his Lord.

In the passage before us, the bride still loves Him truly, though not wholly. There is still a power in His Word that she is aware of, though she no longer renders instant obedience. She little realizes how she is wronging her Lord and how real the wall of separation is between them. To her, worldliness seems only a little thing.

The bride has not realized the solemn truth of many passages in the Word of God that speak in no uncertain terms of the foolishness, the danger, and the sin of friendship with the world. Here are some of these passages:

*Love not the world, neither the things
that are in the world. If any man love
the world, the love of the Father is not in
him.*   *(1 John 2:15)*

*Ye...adulteresses, know ye not that the
friendship of the world is enmity with
God? whosoever therefore will be a
friend of the world is the enemy of God.*
                            (James 4:4)

*Be ye not unequally yoked together with
unbelievers: for what fellowship hath
righteousness with unrighteousness?
and what communion hath light with
darkness? And what concord hath
Christ with Belial? or what part hath he
that believeth with an infidel?...Where-
fore come out from among them, and be
ye separate, saith the Lord, and touch
not the unclean thing; and I will receive
you, and will be a Father unto you, and
ye shall be my sons and daughters, saith
the Lord Almighty.*
                    (2 Cor. 6:14–15, 17–18)

We have to make a choice; we cannot enjoy
both the world and Christ. The bride had not
learned this. She would gladly enjoy both, with
no thought of their incompatibility.

LOVE SEPARATED BY WORLDLINESS

The bride observes the approach of the Bridegroom with joy:

The voice of my beloved! behold, he cometh leaping upon the mountains, skipping upon the hills. My beloved is like a roe or a young hart: behold, he standeth behind our wall, he looketh forth at the windows, showing himself through the lattice. (Song 2:8–9)

The heart of the bride leaps when she hears the voice of her Beloved as He comes in search of her. He has crossed the hills, and He now draws near to her. He stands behind the wall, and He even looks in at the windows. With tender and touching words, He calls her to come to Him. He utters no reproach, and His loving entreaties sink deep in her memory:

My beloved spake, and said unto me, Rise up, my love, my fair one, and come away. For, lo, the winter is past, the rain is over and gone; the flowers appear on the earth; the time of the singing of birds is come, and the voice of the turtle is heard in our land; the fig tree putteth forth her green

> *figs, and the vines with the tender grape*
> *give a good smell. Arise, my love, my fair*
> *one, and come away.*   *(Song 2:10–13)*

The Bridegroom is essentially saying, "All nature is responsive to the return of summer. Will you, My bride, be irresponsive to My love?" *"Arise, my love, my fair one, and come away."* Can such pleading be in vain? Alas, it can, and it was!

In yet more touching words the Bridegroom continues,

> *O my dove, that art in the clefts of the*
> *rock, in the secret places of the stairs, let*
> *me see thy countenance, let me hear thy*
> *voice; for sweet is thy voice, and thy*
> *countenance is comely.*   *(v. 14)*

Wonderful thought, that God should desire fellowship with us, and that He whose love once made Him the Man of Sorrows may now be made the Man of Joys by the loving devotion of human hearts.

But, as strong as His love and His desire for His bride are, He can come no further. He can never come where she is now. But surely she will go forth to Him. Does He not have a claim upon her? She feels and enjoys His love.

Will she let His desire count for nothing? For, let us notice, it is not the bride who is longing in vain for her Lord, but the Bridegroom who is seeking her. It is unfortunate that He should seek in vain! He continues His pleading: *"Take us the foxes, the little foxes, that spoil the vines: for our vines have tender grapes"* (Song 2:15).

A little spray of blossom, so tiny that it can scarcely be perceived, is easily spoiled, but because of this the fruitfulness of a whole branch may forever be destroyed. And how numerous the little foxes are! The enemies may be small, but the mischief that is done is great. Little compromises with the world, disobedience to the still small voice in little things, little indulgences of the flesh to the neglect of duty, doing evil in little things so that good may come—all these things cause the beauty and the fruitfulness of the vine to be sacrificed!

We have a sad illustration of the deceitfulness of sin in the response of the bride. Instead of bounding forth to meet Him, she first comforts her own heart by the remembrance of His faithfulness and of her union with Him: *"My beloved is mine, and I am his: he feedeth among the lilies"* (Song 2:16).

Here, she is basically saying, "My position is one of security. I have no need to be concerned about it. He is mine, and I am His.

39

Nothing can alter that relationship. I can find Him now at any time. He feeds His flock among the lilies. While the sun of prosperity shines upon me, I may safely enjoy myself here without Him. Should trial and darkness come, He will be sure not to fail me."

Until the day break, and the shadows flee away, turn, my beloved, and be thou like a roe or a young hart upon the mountains of Bether.   *(v. 17)*

Careless of His desire, she thus lightly dismisses Him with the thought: "A little later I may enjoy His love." Then, the grieved Bridegroom departs! Poor foolish bride! She will soon find that the things that once satisfied her can satisfy no longer, and that it is easier to turn a deaf ear to His tender call than to recall or find her absent Lord.

The day becomes cool, and the shadows flee away, but He does not return. Then, in the solemn night, she discovers her mistake. It is dark, and she is alone. Retiring to rest, she still hopes for His return, yet the lesson that worldliness is an absolute barrier to full communion is still unlearned: *"By night on my bed I sought him whom my soul loveth: I sought him, but I found him not"* (Song 3:1).

She waits and becomes weary. His absence becomes unbearable:

I will rise now, and go about the city in the streets, and in the broad ways I will seek him whom my soul loveth: I sought him, but I found him not. (v. 2)

How different her position is now from what it might have been! Instead of seeking Him while she is alone, desolate, and in the dark, she might have gone forth with Him in the sunshine, leaning upon His arm. Instead of the partial view of her Beloved through the lattice, where she could no longer say "There is nothing between us," she might have had the joy of His embrace and His public confession of her as His chosen bride!

The watchmen that go about the city found me: to whom I said, Saw ye him whom my soul loveth? It was but a little that I passed from them, but I found him whom my soul loveth. (vv. 3–4)

She has obeyed His command, *"Arise...and come away"* (Song 2:13). Fearless of reproach, she was seeking Him in the dark, and when she began to confess Him as her Lord, she soon found Him and was restored to His favor:

*I held him, and would not let him go,
until I had brought him into my
mother's house, and into the chamber of
her that conceived me.* (Song 3:4)

Jerusalem above is *"the mother of us all"*
(Gal. 4:26). That is where communion is enjoyed, but not in worldly ways or self-willed
indulgence.

LOVE RESTORED

Communion having been fully restored,
this section of Song of Solomon closes, as did
the first, with the loving charge of the Bridegroom that no one should disturb His bride:

*I charge you, O ye daughters of Jerusa-
lem, by the roes, and by the hinds of the
field,* [by all that is loving and beautiful
and constant] *that ye stir not up, nor
awake my love, till* [she] *please.*
(Song 3:5)

May we all, while living here as in the
world but not of it, find our home in the heav-
enly places in which we are seated together
with Christ (Eph. 2:6). As we are sent into the
world to witness for our Master, may we always

be strangers there, ready to confess Him as the true object of our soul's devotion.

> *How amiable are thy tabernacles, O LORD of hosts! My soul longeth, yea, even fainteth for the courts of the LORD: my heart and my flesh crieth out for the living God....Blessed are they that dwell in thy house: they will be still praising thee....A day in thy courts is better than a thousand. I had rather be a doorkeeper in the house of my God, than to dwell in the tents of wickedness. For the LORD God is a sun and shield: the LORD will give grace and glory: no good thing will he withhold from them that walk uprightly. O LORD of hosts, blessed is the man that trusteth in thee.*
> *(Ps. 84:1–2, 4, 10–12)*

Chapter 4

The Joy of Unbroken Communion

Song of Solomon 3:6–5:1

We have been mainly occupied in the last two sections of the Song of Solomon with the words and the experiences of the bride. In marked contrast to this, our attention in this section is first called to the Bridegroom, and it is from Him that we hear of the bride as the object of His love and the delight of His heart.

The daughters of Jerusalem are the first speakers:

> *Who is this that cometh up out of the wilderness like pillars of smoke, perfumed with myrrh and frankincense, with all powders of the merchant?*
> *(Song 3:6)*

They themselves give the reply:

> *King Solomon made himself a chariot of the wood of Lebanon. He made the pillars thereof of silver, the bottom thereof of gold, the covering of it of purple, the midst thereof being paved with love,* [love gifts from] *the daughters of Jerusalem....Behold his bed, which is Solomon's; threescore valiant men are about it, of the valiant of Israel. They all hold swords, being expert in war: every man hath his sword upon his thigh because of fear in the night.*   *(vv. 9–10, 7–8)*

ALL GLORY FOR THE BRIDEGROOM

In the above verses the bride is not mentioned. She is eclipsed in the grandeur and the state of her royal Bridegroom; nevertheless, she is both enjoying and sharing it. The very air is perfumed by the smoke of the incense that ascends, pillarlike, to the clouds, and all that protects the position of the Bridegroom Himself and shows forth His dignity also protects the accompanying bride, the sharer of His glory.

The chariot in which they sit is built of fragrant cedar from Lebanon, and the finest of gold and silver have been used in its construction. The fragrant wood typifies the beauty of sanctified humanity, while the gold reminds us of the divine glory of our Lord, and the silver of the purity and preciousness of His redeemed and peerless church. The imperial purple with which it is lined tells us of the Gentiles—the daughter of Tyre has been there with her gift (Ps. 45:12). And the love gifts of the daughters of Jerusalem are in accord with the prophecy, *"even the rich among the people shall entreat thy favour"* (v. 12).

These are the things that attract the attention of the daughters of Jerusalem, but the bride is occupied with the King Himself, and she exclaims,

> *Go forth, O ye daughters of Zion, and behold king Solomon with the crown wherewith his mother crowned him in the day of his espousals, and in the day of the gladness of his heart.* (Song 3:11)

The crowned King is everything to the bride, and she would have Him to be so to the daughters of Zion as well. She delights in the gladness of His heart on the day of His betrothal, for now she is not occupied with Him for her own sake, but rejoices in His joy in finding His satisfaction in her.

Do we sufficiently cultivate this unselfish desire to be all for Jesus and to do all for His pleasure? Or are we conscious that we principally go to Him for our own sakes, or at best for the sake of our fellowmen? How much prayer there is that begins and ends with created man, that is forgetful of the privilege of giving joy to the Creator! Yet, it is only when He sees in our unselfish love and devotion to Him the reflection of His own love and devotion that His heart can feel full satisfaction and pour itself forth in precious utterances of love. We find this in the following words:

> *Behold, thou art fair, my love; behold, thou art fair; thou hast doves' eyes within thy locks: thy hair is as a flock of goats, that appear from mount Gilead. Thy teeth are like a flock of sheep that are even shorn, which came up from the washing; whereof every one bear twins, and none is barren among them. Thy lips are like a thread of scarlet, and thy speech is comely: thy temples are like a piece of pomegranate within thy locks. Thy neck is like the tower of David builded for an armoury, whereon there hang a thousand bucklers, all shields of mighty men. Thy two breasts are like two young roes that are twins, which feed among the lilies.*
>
> *(Song 4:1–3)*

We have already found the explanation of the fairness of the bride in her reflecting, like a mirror, the beauty of the Bridegroom. He may well describe her beauty with satisfaction while she is thus occupied with Him! The lips that speak only of Him are like a thread of scarlet. The mouth, or speech, that has no word of self, or for self, is pleasing in His sight.

We can well imagine how sweet His words of appreciation and commendation are to the bride, but her joy is too deep for expression. She is silent in her love. She would not now think of sending Him away until the day becomes cool and the shadows flee away.

LOVE FOR THE BRIDE

Still less does the Bridegroom think of finding His joy apart from His bride. He says, *"Until the day break, and the shadows flee away, I will get me to the mountain of myrrh, and to the hill of frankincense"* (Song 4:6).

Separation never originates with Him. He is always ready for communion with a prepared heart, and in this happy communion the bride becomes fairer and more like her Lord. She is being changed progressively into His image through the wondrous working of the

Holy Spirit, from one degree of glory to another. Because of this transformation, the Bridegroom can declare, *"Thou art all fair, my love; there is no spot in thee"* (v. 7).

Now she is fit for service, and the Bridegroom woos her to such service. She will not now misrepresent Him.

> *Come with me from Lebanon, my* [bride], *with me from Lebanon: look from the top of Amana, from the top of Shenir and Hermon, from the lions' dens, from the mountains of the leopards.* (Song 4:8)

"Come with me." It is always so. If our Savior says, *"Go ye therefore, and teach all nations"* (Matt. 28:19), He precedes it with, *"All power is given unto me"* (v. 18) and follows it with, *"Lo, I am with you alway"* (v. 20). Or if, as it is here, He calls His bride to come, it is still *"with me,"* and it is in connection with this loving invitation that for the first time He exchanges the words "My love" for the still more endearing ones, "My bride" or "My spouse."

What are lions' dens when the Lion of the tribe of Judah is with us, or mountains of leopards when He is at our side? *"I will fear no evil:*

for thou art with me" (Ps. 23:4). On the other
hand, it is while the bride is thus facing dangers
and toiling with Him in service that He says the
following:

> *Thou hast ravished my heart, my sister,
> my* [bride]; *thou hast ravished my heart
> with one of thine eyes, with one chain of
> thy neck.*   *(Song 4:9)*

It is wonderful how the heart of our Beloved can be ravished so with the love of one
who is prepared to accept His invitation and go
forth with Him, seeking to rescue the perishing! The marginal note for verse four in the
Revised Version is very significant. The phrase
may be translated, *"Thou hast given me courage."*

If the Bridegroom's heart may be encour-
aged by the fidelity and loving companionship
of His bride, it is not surprising that we may
cheer and encourage one another in our mutual service. Paul had a steep mountain of difficulty to climb when he was being led as a
captive to Rome, not knowing the things that
awaited him there. But when the believers met
him at the Appii forum, he thanked God and
took courage (Acts 28:15). May we always so
strengthen one another in God!

FULL CONSECRATION OF SELF

The Bridegroom cheers those who take the toilsome way and the steep path of danger, with sweet communications of His love:

> *How fair is thy love, my sister, my [bride]! how much better is thy love than wine! and the smell of thine ointments than all spices! Thy lips, O my [bride], drop as the honeycomb: honey and milk are under thy tongue; and the smell of thy garments is like the smell of Lebanon. A garden enclosed is my sister, my [bride]; a spring shut up, a fountain sealed. Thy plants are an orchard of pomegranates, with pleasant fruits; camphire, with spikenard, spikenard and saffron; calamus and cinnamon, with all trees of frankincense; myrrh and aloes, with all the chief spices: a fountain of gardens, a well of living waters, and streams from Lebanon.*
>
> *(Song 4:10–15)*

Since the bride is engaged with the Bridegroom in seeking to rescue the perishing, the utterances of her lips are like honey and the honeycomb to Him, and He piles metaphor upon metaphor to express His satisfaction and

joy. She is a garden full of precious fruits and
delightful perfumes, but a garden enclosed.
The fruit she bears may bring blessing to
many, but the garden is only for the Bridegroom. She is a fountain, but a spring shut up,
a fountain sealed. And yet again she is a fountain of gardens, a well of living waters and
flowing streams from Lebanon. She carries fer-
tility and imparts refreshment wherever she
goes, and yet it is all of Him and for Him.

The bride now speaks for the second time
in this section. Since as her first utterance was
of Him, her second is now for Him; self is
found in neither.

> *Awake, O north wind; and come, thou*
> *south; blow upon my garden, that the*
> *spices thereof may flow out. Let my be-*
> *loved come into his garden, and eat his*
> *pleasant fruits.*   (Song 4:16)

She is ready for any experience. The north
wind and the south may blow upon her garden,
if only the spices from it may flow out to delight her Lord by their fragrance. He has called
her His garden, a paradise of pomegranates
and precious fruits. Let Him come into it and
eat His precious fruits.

To this the Bridegroom replies with the
following:

I am come into my garden, my sister, my
[bride]: I have gathered my myrrh with
my spice; I have eaten my honeycomb
with my honey; I have drunk my wine
with my milk.   *(Song 5:1)*

Now when she calls, He answers at once.
When she is living only for her Lord, He as-
sures her that He finds all His satisfaction in
her.

This section of the Song of Solomon closes
with the bride's invitation to the Bridegroom's
friends and to her friends, as well as to the
Bridegroom: *"Eat, O friends; drink, yea, drink*
abundantly, O beloved" (Song 5:1).

Far from lessening our power to impart
power and joy, the consecration of all to our
Master increases both our power and our joy as
we minister. The five loaves and two fishes of
the disciples, which were first given up to and
blessed by the Lord, were an abundant supply
for the needy multitudes. They grew, in the act
of distribution, into a supply of which twelve
baskets full of leftovers remained, even after
all had had plenty to eat.

We have, then, in this beautiful section, a
picture of unbroken communion and its delightful results. May our lives correspond to
this! First, let us be one with the King; then let

us speak of the King. The joy of communion should lead us to fellowship in service, to living completely for Jesus, ready for any experience that will equip us for further service. It should help us to surrender all to Him and be willing to minister all for Him. There is no room for love of the world here, for union with Christ has filled the heart. There is nothing for the gratification of the world here, for all has been sealed and is kept for the Master's use.

> Jesus, my life is Thine!
> And evermore shall be
>   Hidden in Thee.
> For nothing can untwine
> Thy life from mine.

> O Jesu, King most wonderful,
>   Thou Conqueror renown'd.
> Thou sweetness most ineffable,
>   In whom all joys are found!
> Thee, Jesu, may our voices bless;
>   Thee may we love alone;
> And ever in our lives express
>   The image of Thine own.

Chapter 5

Restored Once More

Song of Solomon 5:2–6:10

The fourth section of the Song of Solomon commences with an address of the bride to the daughters of Jerusalem. In this address, she narrates her recent sad experience and asks for their help in her trouble. The presence and comfort of her Bridegroom are again lost to her, not this time by relapse into worldliness, but by slothful self-indulgence.

We are not told of the steps that led to her failure, of how self again found place in her heart. Perhaps spiritual pride in the achievements that grace enabled her to accomplish was the cause. Or, possibly, a cherished satisfaction in the *blessing* she had received, instead of in the *Blesser* Himself, may have led to the separation. She seems to have been largely unconscious of her downfall. While she was self-occupied and self-contented, she scarcely noticed His absence. She was resting alone, never asking where He had gone or what He was doing. And, more than this, the door of her chamber was not only closed, but barred, an evidence that His return was neither eagerly desired nor expected.

Yet her heart was not far from Him. There was a music in His voice that awakened echoes in her soul that no other voice could have stirred. She was still *"a garden enclosed...a fountain sealed"* (Song 4:12) as far as the world was concerned. The snare this time was more dangerous and insidious because it was quite unsuspected. Her narrative is as follows:

> *I sleep, but my heart waketh: it is the voice of my beloved that knocketh, saying, Open to me, my sister, my love, my dove, my undefiled: for my head is filled with dew, and my locks with the drops of the night.* (Song 5:2)

A KNOCKING SUITOR

How often the position of the Bridegroom is that of a suitor who is outside knocking, as in His letter to the Laodicean church: *"Behold, I stand at the door, and knock: if any man hear*

my voice, and open the door, I will come in to
him, and will sup with him, and he with me"
(Rev. 3:20). It is sad that He should be outside
a closed door, that He should need to knock.
But it is still more sad that He should knock,
and knock in vain, at the door of any heart
that has become His own. In this case, it is not
the location of the bride that is wrong. If it
were, His word would be, as before, *"Arise...
and come away"* (Song 2:13), whereas now His
word is, *"Open to me, my sister, my love, my
dove, my undefiled"* (5:2). It was her condition
of self-satisfaction and love of ease that closed
the door.

His words are very touching: *"'Open to me,
my sister,'* for I am the firstborn among many
brothers; *'my love,'* the object of My heart's
devotion; *'my dove,'* one who has been endued
with many of the gifts and graces of the Holy
Spirit; *'my undefiled,'* washed, renewed, and
cleansed for Me." The Bridegroom then urges
her, by reference to His own condition, to open
to Him: *"My head is filled with dew, and my
locks with the drops of the night"* (v. 2).

Why is it that His head is filled with the
dew? Because His heart is a shepherd's heart.
There are those whom the Father has given to
Him who are wandering on the dark mountains
of sin. Many have never heard the Shepherd's

voice. Many, too, who once were in the fold have wandered away, far away from its safe shelter. The heart that can never forget, the love that can never fail, must seek the wandering sheep until the lost one has been found: *"My Father worketh hitherto, and I work"* (John 5:17). And will she, who was so recently at His side, who joyfully braved the dens of lions and the mountains of leopards, will she leave Him to seek the wandering and the lost by Himself? *"Open to me, my sister, my love, my dove, my undefiled: for my head is filled with dew, and my locks with the drops of the night"* (Song 5:2). I do not know of a more touching entreaty in the Word of God, and the reply of the bride is sad, indeed: *"I have put off my coat; how shall I put it on? I have washed my feet; how shall I defile them?"* (v. 3).

How sadly possible it is to take delight in Bible conferences and customs, to feast on all the good things that are brought before us, and yet to be unprepared to go out from them to self-denying efforts to rescue the perishing. Unfortunately, it is possible to delight in faith's rest while forgetting to fight the good fight of faith, to dwell upon the cleansing and the purity effected by faith, but to have little thought for the poor souls struggling in the mire of sin. If we can take off our coats when

He wants us to keep them on, if we can wash our feet while He is wandering alone upon the mountains, is there not a sad lack of fellowship with our Lord?

SELFISH DISOBEDIENCE

Meeting with no response from the tardy bride, her *"beloved put in his hand by the hole of the door, and* [her heart was] *moved for him"* (Song 5:4). But, alas, the door was not only latched, but barred, and His effort to secure an entrance was in vain.

> *I rose up to open to my beloved; and my hands dropped with myrrh, and my fingers with sweet smelling myrrh, upon the handles of the lock. I opened to my beloved; but my beloved had withdrawn himself, and was gone: my soul failed when he spake.* (vv. 5–6)

When the bride did arise all too late, she seems to have been more concerned about anointing herself with the liquid myrrh than about welcoming her waiting Lord speedily. She seems more occupied with her own graces than with His desire. No words of welcome were uttered, though her heart failed within her, and the grieved One had withdrawn Himself before she was ready to receive Him. Again, as in the third chapter of the Song of Solomon, she has to go forth alone to seek her Lord. This time her experiences are much more painful than on the former occasion:

I sought him, but I could not find him; I called him, but he gave me no answer. The watchmen that went about the city found me, they smote me, they wounded me; the keepers of the walls took away my veil from me. (Song 5:6–7)

Her first relapse had been one of inexperience. If the second relapse had been brought about by inattention, at least she would have been ready and prompt when summoned to obey. It is not a little thing to fall into the habit of being tardy in obedience, even in the case of a believer. In the case of an unbeliever, the final result of disobedience is inexpressibly awful:

Turn you at my reproof: behold, I will pour out my spirit unto you, I will make known my words unto you. Because I have called, and ye refused; I have stretched out my hand, and no man regarded....I also will laugh at your calamity....Then shall they call upon me,

> *but I will not answer; they shall seek me*
> *early, but they shall not find me.*
> > *(Prov. 1:23–24, 26, 28)*

REPENTANCE AND REPROACH

The backsliding of the bride, though painful, was not final, for it was followed by true
repentance. She went forth into the darkness
and sought Him. She called, but He did not re-
spond. She was both struck and wounded by
the watchmen who found her. They appear to
have appreciated the gravity of her downfall
more correctly than she had. Believers may be
blinded to their own inconsistencies. Others,
however, see them, and the more visible believers are with regard to our Lord, the more
surely any failure will be visited with reproach.

Wounded, dishonored, unsuccessful in her
search, and almost in despair, the bride turns
to the daughters of Jerusalem. As she recounts
the story of her sorrows, she begs them to tell
her Beloved that she is not unfaithful or unmindful of Him. *"I charge you, O daughters of
Jerusalem, if ye find my beloved, that ye tell
him, that I am sick of love"* (Song 5:8).

The reply of the daughters of Jerusalem
shows very clearly that the sorrowful bride,
wandering in the dark, is not recognized as the

bride of the King, though her personal beauty does not escape notice.

> *What is thy beloved more than another beloved, O thou fairest among women? what is thy beloved more than another beloved, that thou dost so charge us?*
>
> *(v. 9)*

This question, implying that her Beloved is no more important than any other, stirs the bride's soul to its deepest depths. Forgetting herself, she pours out from the fullness of her heart a soul-ravishing description of the glory and beauty of her Lord.

> *My beloved is white and ruddy, the chiefest among ten thousand. His head is as the most fine gold, his locks are bushy, and black as a raven. His eyes are as the eyes of doves by the rivers of waters, washed with milk, and fitly set. His cheeks are as a bed of spices, as sweet flowers: his lips like lilies, dropping sweet smelling myrrh. His hands are as gold rings set with the beryl: his belly is as bright ivory overlaid with sapphires. His legs are as pillars of marble, set upon sockets of fine gold: his countenance is as Lebanon, excellent as*

the cedars. His mouth is most sweet: yea, he is altogether lovely. This is my beloved, and this is my friend, O daughters of Jerusalem.   *(vv. 10–16)*

It is interesting to compare the bride's description of the Bridegroom with the description of the Ancient of Days in Daniel 7:9–10:

I beheld till the thrones were cast down, and the Ancient of days did sit, whose garment was white as snow, and the hair of his head like the pure wool: his throne was like the fiery flame, and his wheels as burning fire. A fiery stream issued and came forth from before him: thousand thousands ministered unto him, and ten thousand times ten thousand stood before him: the judgment was set, and the books were opened.

It is also possible to compare this passage from the Song of Solomon with the description of our risen Lord in Revelation 1:13–16:

And in the midst of the seven candlesticks one like unto the Son of man, clothed with a garment down to the foot, and girt about the paps with a golden girdle. His head and his hairs were white like wool, as white as snow; and his eyes were as a flame of fire; and his feet like unto fine brass, as if they burned in a furnace; and his voice as the sound of many waters. And he had in his right hand seven stars: and out of his mouth went a sharp twoedged sword: and his countenance was as the sun shineth in his strength.

The differences between the passage in Song of Solomon and the passages in Daniel and Revelation are very characteristic.

In Daniel chapter seven, the Ancient of Days was described as being seated on the throne of judgment. His garment was white as snow, and the hair on His head was like pure wool. His throne and His wheels were like burning fire, and a fiery stream came forth from before Him. The Son of Man was brought before Him and received from Him dominion, glory, and an everlasting kingdom that will not be destroyed.

In Revelation chapter one, the Son of Man Himself was described as being clothed with a garment down to His feet, and His head and His hair were white as wool or as snow. But the bride sees her Bridegroom in all the vigor of youth; His hair is *"bushy, and black as a raven"* (Song 5:11). The eyes of the risen Savior were described as *"a flame of fire"* (Rev. 1:14), but His bride sees them like *"doves by the rivers of waters"* (Song 5:12). In Revelation, His voice was *"as the sound of many waters...and out of his mouth went a sharp twoedged sword"* (vv. 15–16). To the bride, His lips are like lilies, dripping liquid myrrh, and His mouth is most sweet.

The countenance of the risen Savior was *"as the sun shineth in his strength"* (Rev. 1:16), and the effect of the vision on John— *"when I saw him, I fell at his feet as dead"* (v. 17)—was not unlike the effect of the vision given to Saul as he neared Damascus. But to His bride, His *"countenance is as Lebanon, excellent as the cedars"* (Song 5:15). The Lion of the Tribe of Judah is to His own bride the King of Love. With full heart and beaming face, the bride recounts His beauties in such a way that the daughters of Jerusalem are seized with a strong desire to seek Him with her, so that they also may behold His beauty.

> *Whither is thy beloved gone, O thou fairest among women? whither is thy beloved turned aside? that we may seek him with thee?* (Song 6:1)

The bride replies with the following:

> *My beloved is gone down into his gar-*
> *den, to the beds of spices, to feed in the*
> *gardens, and to gather lilies. I am my*
> *beloved's, and my beloved is mine: he*
> *feedeth among the lilies.* (vv. 2–3)

A RESTORED BRIDE

Even though she might appear forlorn and
desolate, she still knows that she is the object
of His affections, and she claims Him as her
own. This expression, *"I am my beloved's, and
my beloved is mine,"* is similar to the one found
in the second chapter of the Song of Solomon,
"My beloved is mine, and I am his" (v. 16), yet
with noteworthy difference. Then, her first
thought of Christ was of her claim upon Him;
His claim upon her was secondary. Now she
thinks first of His claim, and only afterwards
does she mention her own. We see a still further development of grace in Song of Solomon
7:10, where the bride, losing sight of her claim
altogether, says, *"I am my beloved's, and his
desire is toward me."*

No sooner has she uttered the words at the
beginning of chapter six, and acknowledged
herself as His rightful possession—a claim that
she had practically repudiated when she kept

Him barred out—than her Bridegroom Himself appears. With no upbraiding word, but in tenderest love, He tells her how beautiful she is in His eyes, and speaks her praise to the daughters of Jerusalem. He says to her,

Thou art beautiful, O my love, as Tirzah [the beautiful city of Samaria], *comely as Jerusalem* [the glorious city of the great King], *terrible* [that is, brilliant] *as an army with banners. Turn away thine eyes from me, for they have overcome me: thy hair is as a flock of goats that appear from Gilead. Thy teeth are as a flock of sheep which go up from the washing, whereof every one beareth twins, and there is not one barren among them. As a piece of a pomegranate are thy temples within thy locks.*

(Song 6:4–7)

Then, turning to the daughters of Jerusalem, He exclaims,

There are threescore queens, and fourscore concubines, and virgins without number. My dove, my undefiled is but one; she is the only one of her mother, she is the choice one of her that bare her. The daughters saw her, and blessed her;

67

*yea, the queens and the concubines, and
they praised her. Who is she that looketh
forth as the morning, fair as the moon,
clear as the sun, and terrible as an army
with banners?*   *(vv. 8–10)*

Thus the section closes with communion
fully restored. The bride has been reinstated
and openly acknowledged by the Bridegroom
as His own peerless companion and friend. The
painful experience through which the bride
has passed has been filled with lasting good,
and we have no further indication of interrupted communion. In the remaining sections,
there is only joy and fruitfulness.

Chapter 6

Fruits of Recognized Union

Song of Solomon 6:11–8:4

*I*n the second and fourth sections of Song of Solomon (chapters three and five of this book), we found the communion of the bride broken. In the second section, it was due to backsliding into worldliness, and in the fourth section, it was due to slothful ease and self-satisfaction. The present section, like the third, is one of unbroken communion. It is opened by the words of the bride:

> *I went down into the garden of nuts to see the fruits of the valley, and to see whether the vine flourished, and the pomegranates budded. Or ever I was aware, my soul made me like the chariots of Amminadib* [my willing people].
> *(Song 6:11–12)*

ONE WITH THE BRIDEGROOM

In the beginning of section three, the bride, in unbroken communion with her Lord, was present though unmentioned until she made her presence evident by her address to the daughters of Zion. In this section, the presence of the King is not noted until He Himself addresses His bride. But she is one with her Lord as she engages in His service.

His promise, *"Lo, I am with you alway"* (Matt. 28:20), is always fulfilled for her. He no longer has to woo her to arise and come away, to tell her that His *"head is filled with dew,"* His *"locks with the drops of the night"* (Song 5:2). He does not need to urge her, if she loves Him, to feed His sheep and care for His lambs (John 21:15–17).

Since the bride is in the Bridegroom's garden, she does not forget to tend it, or keep the vineyards of others while her own is neglected. *With* Him as well as *for* Him, she goes to the garden of nuts. The union between them is so thorough that many commentators have had difficulty in deciding whether the bride or the Bridegroom was the speaker. It is really a point of little matter, because, as I have said, both were there and of one mind. Yet I believe I am correct in attributing these words to the bride, since she is the one addressed by the daughters of Jerusalem and the one who speaks to them in reply.

The bride and Bridegroom appear to have been discovered by their willing people while engaged in the happy fellowship of fruitful service. The bride, before she was aware, found herself seated among the chariots of her people—her people as well as His.

The daughters of Jerusalem would gladly call her back: *"Return, return, O Shulamite; return, return, that we may look upon thee"* (Song 6:13). There is no question now as to who she is or why her Beloved is more than another beloved. He is recognized as King Solomon, and the same name is given to her, only in its feminine form (Shulamite).

The bride replies to the daughters of Jerusalem with the following: *"What will ye see in the Shulamite?"* (v. 13). In the presence of the King, she cannot comprehend why any attention should be paid to her. As Moses, coming down from the mount, was unconscious that his face shone with a divine glory, so it is here with the bride. But we may learn this very important lesson, that many who do not see the beauty of the Lord will not fail to admire His reflected beauty in His bride. The eager look of the daughters of Jerusalem surprised the bride, and she says to them, "You could be looking on *'the company of two armies'* (v. 13)"—the dance of two companies of Israel's fairest daughters—instead of on one who has no claim for attention, except that she is the chosen, though unworthy, bride of the glorious King.

The daughters of Jerusalem have no difficulty in replying to her question and recognizing her as being of royal birth as well as of queenly dignity: *"O Prince's daughter!"* (Song 7:1). They describe in true and Oriental language the tenfold beauties of her person:

> *How beautiful are thy feet with shoes, O prince's daughter! the joints of thy thighs are like jewels, the work of the hands of a cunning workman. Thy navel is like a round goblet, which wanteth not liquor: thy belly is like an heap of wheat set about with lilies. Thy two breasts are like two young roes that are twins. Thy neck is as a tower of ivory; thine eyes like the fishpools in Heshbon, by the gate of Bathrabbim: thy nose is as the tower of Lebanon which looketh toward Damascus. Thine head upon thee is like Carmel, and the hair of thine head like purple; the king is held in the galleries.*
>
> *(Song 7:1–5)*

From her head to her feet they see only beauty and perfection. What a contrast to her natural state! Once, *"from the sole of the foot even unto the head"* were *"but wounds, and bruises, and putrifying sores"* (Isa. 1:6), but now her feet are *"shod with the preparation of the gospel of peace"* (Eph. 6:15). The very hair of her head proclaims her to be a Nazarite indeed; *"the king"* Himself *"is held in the galleries"* because of *"the hair of* [her] *head"* (Song 7:5).

But there is One who means more to her than the daughters of Jerusalem, and He, the Bridegroom Himself, responds to her simple question, *"What will ye see in the Shulamite?"* (Song 6:13), in the following way: *"How fair and how pleasant art thou, O love, for delights!"* (Song 7:6).

FLOURISHING RIGHTEOUSNESS

The Bridegroom sees in the bride the beauty and the fruitfulness of the tall and upright palm, of the graceful and clinging vine, and of the fragrant and evergreen apple. Grace has made her like the palm tree, the emblem of both uprightness and fruitfulness: *"This thy stature is like to a palm tree"* (Song 7:7).

The fruit of the date palm is more valued than bread by the Oriental traveler because of its great sustaining power, and the fruit-bearing powers of the tree do not pass away. As the age of the tree increases, the fruit becomes more perfect as well as more abundant.

> *The righteous shall flourish like the palm tree: he shall grow like a cedar in Lebanon. Those that be planted in the house of the LORD shall flourish in the courts of our God. They shall still bring forth fruit in old age; they shall be fat and flourishing.* (Ps. 92:12–14)

But why are the righteous made so upright and flourishing? *"To show that the LORD is upright; he is my rock, and there is no unrighteousness in him"* (v. 15). Being one with the Lord, it is the responsibility of the righteous to show forth His graces and virtues, to reflect His beauty, and to be His faithful witnesses.

The palm is also the emblem of victory. It raises its beautiful crown toward the heavens, fearless of the heat of the sultry sun or of the burning hot wind from the desert. Because of its beauty, it was one of the ornaments of Solomon's temple. It was also described as an ornament of the temple described in the book of Ezekiel. When our Savior was received as

the King of Israel in Jerusalem, the people
took branches of palm trees and went forth to
meet Him. In the glorious day of His betrothal,
"a great multitude, which no man [can] *number, of all nations, and kindreds, and people,
and tongues,* [will stand] *before the throne, and
before the Lamb, clothed with white robes,* [and
with palms of victory in their hands, they will
exclaim]*...Salvation to our God which sitteth
upon the throne, and unto the Lamb"* (Rev.
7:9–10).

But if the bride resembles the palm, she
also resembles the vine: *"Now also thy breasts
shall be as clusters of the vine"* (Song 7:8). She
much needs the cultivating of the Farmer, and
she repays Him well for it. Abiding in Christ,
who is the true source of fruitfulness, she
brings forth clusters of grapes that are luscious
and refreshing, as well as sustaining, like the
fruit of the palm. These grapes are luscious
and refreshing to Him, the owner of the vineyard, as well as to the weary, thirsty world in
which He has placed it.

The image of the vine suggests some important lessons. It needs and seeks support.
The sharp knife of the one who prunes often
cuts away its tender garlands unsparingly and
mars its appearance while increasing its fruitfulness. It has been beautifully written:

One with Christ

The living Vine, Christ chose it for Himself:
God gave to man for use and sustenance
Corn, wine, and oil, and each of these is good:
And Christ is Bread of life and Light of life.
But yet, He did not choose the summer corn,
That shoots up straight and free in one quick growth,
And has its day, is done, and springs no more;
Nor yet the olive, all whose boughs are spread
In the soft air, and never lose a leaf,
Flowering and fruitful in perpetual peace;
But only this, for Him and His is one,
That everlasting, ever-quickening Vine,
That gives the heat and passion of the world,
Through its own life-blood, still renewed and shed.

The Vine from every living limb bleeds wine;
Is it the poorer for that spirit shed?
The drunkard and the wanton drink thereof;
Are they the richer for that gift's excess?
Measure thy life by loss instead of gain;
Not by the wine drunk, but the wine poured forth;
For love's strength standeth in love's sacrifice;
And whoso suffers most, hath most to give.

Yet, besides the palm and the vine, one
more metaphor is used by the Bridegroom:
"The smell of thy nose [is] *like apples"* (Song
7:8). In the first section, the bride exclaimed,

> *As the apple tree among the trees of the*
> *wood, so is my beloved among the sons. I*
> *sat down under his shadow with great*

> *delight, and his fruit was sweet to my*
> *taste.*   *(Song 2:3)*

Here we find the outcome of that communion. The apples on which she had fed perfumed her breath and imparted to her their delicious scent.

The Bridegroom concludes His description with, *"The roof of thy mouth* [is] *like the best wine,"* and the bride interjects, *"causing the lips of those that are asleep to speak"* (Song 7:9).

NO MORE OF SELF

How wondrous is the grace that has made the bride of Christ to be all this to her Beloved! She is as upright as the palm, victorious, and forevermore fruitful as she grows heavenward. She has become gentle and tender as the vine, self-forgetful and self-sacrificing, not merely bearing fruit in spite of adversity, but bearing her richest fruit through it. She is feasting on her Beloved as she rests beneath His shade, and thereby she is partaking of His fragrance. What has grace not done for her! And what must be her joy in finding, ever more fully, the satisfaction that the glorious Bridegroom has in the lowly wildflower that He has transformed into His bride! He has indeed made her beautiful with His own graces and virtues! Because of this, she gladly exclaims, *"I am my beloved's, and his desire is toward me"* (Song 7:10).

Now it is none of self or for self, but all of the Lord and for the Lord. And if these are the sweet fruits of going down to the garden of nuts and caring for His garden with Him, the bride will need no coercion to continue in this blessed service: *"Come, my beloved, let us go forth into the field; let us lodge in the villages"* (v. 11).

The bride is not ashamed of her lowly origin, for she fears no shame. Perfect love has cast out fear. The royal state of the King, with its pomp and grandeur, may be enjoyed before long. Now it is more sweet to have Him at her side to make the garden fruitful. She is able to give to Him all kinds of precious fruits, new and old, that she has laid up for Him. Best of all, she can satisfy Him with her own love. Not only is she contented with this fellowship of service, but she would gladly wish that there were no honors and duties to claim His attention and for the moment to lessen the joy of His presence.

> *O that thou wert as my brother, that sucked the breasts of my mother! when I should find thee without, I would kiss thee; yea, I should not be despised.*
>
> *(Song 8:1)*

If only she could care for Him and claim His whole attention, as a sister might care for a brother. She is deeply conscious that He has richly endowed her and that she is as nothing compared with Him. But instead of proudly dwelling upon what she has done through Him, she would prefer that it would be possible for her to be the giver and Him the receiver. This is far removed from the grudging thought that must grate so on the heart of our Lord, "I do not think that God requires this of me" or, "Must I give up that, if I am to be a Christian?" True devotion would instead ask to be allowed to give and would count as loss all that may not be given up for the Lord's sake: *"I count all things but loss for the excellency of the knowledge of Christ Jesus my Lord"* (Phil. 3:8).

This desire to be more to Him does not, however, blind her to the consciousness that she needs His guidance and that He is her true and only Instructor.

> *I would lead thee, and bring thee into my mother's house, who would instruct me: I would cause thee to drink of spiced wine of the juice of my pomegranate.*
> *(Song 8:2)*

She is essentially saying, "I want to give You my best, and yet I want to seek all my rest

79

and satisfaction in You." *"His left hand should be under my head, and his right hand should embrace me"* (v. 3).

This is how the section closes. There is nothing sweeter to the Bridegroom or to the bride than this hallowed and unhindered communion. Then He again advises the daughters of Jerusalem, in a slightly different form: *"I charge you, O daughters of Jerusalem, that ye stir not up, nor awake my love, until* [she] *please"* (v. 4).

Hallowed communion, indeed! May we always enjoy it, and while we are abiding in Christ, we will sing, like the familiar words of the well-known hymn:

> Both Thine arms are clasped around me,
>   And my head is on Thy breast;
> And my weary soul hath found Thee
>   Such a perfect, perfect rest!
>   Blessed Jesus,
>   Now I know that I am blest.

Chapter 7

Final Oneness

Song of Solomon 8:5–14

I have now reached the closing section of the Song of Solomon, which, as I have shown, is a poem describing the life of a believer on earth.

Beginning in section one (Song 1:2–2:7) with the unsatisfied longings of a betrothed one—longings that could only be met by the bride's unreserved surrender to the Bridegroom of her soul—we find that when the surrender was made, she found a King instead of the cross she had so much feared. This King is the King of Love, who both satisfied her deepest longings and found His own satisfaction in her.

The second section (Song 2:8–3:5) showed failure on the bride's part. She was lured back again into the world and soon found that her Beloved could not follow her there. Then, with full purpose of heart, going forth to seek Him and confessing His name, her search was successful and her communion was restored.

The third section (Song 3:6–5:1) tells of unbroken communion. Abiding in Christ, the bride was the sharer of His security and His glory. However, she drew the attention of the daughters of Jerusalem from these outward aspects to her King Himself. And, while she was thus occupied with Him, and would have others so occupied, she found that her royal Bridegroom was delighting in her and inviting her to fellowship of service, service in which she would be fearless of dens of lions and mountains of leopards.

The fourth section (Song 5:2–6:10), however, shows failure again, not as before through worldliness, but rather through spiritual pride and sloth. Here restoration was much more difficult. But again, when the bride went forth diligently to seek her Lord, and so confessed Him in a way that led others to long to find Him with her, He revealed Himself, and the communion was restored, to be interrupted no more.

The fifth section (Song 6:11–8:4) not only describes the mutual satisfaction and delight of the bride and Bridegroom in each other, but also the recognition of her position and her beauty by the daughters of Jerusalem.

And now, in the sixth section (Song 8:5–14), we come to the closing scene of the book. In it, the bride is seen leaning upon her Beloved, asking Him to bind her yet more firmly to Himself. She is seen occupying herself in His vineyard until He calls her away from earthly service.

A LOVING BOND

This last section opens, as did the third, by an inquiry or exclamation of the daughters of Jerusalem. In section three they asked, *"Who is this that cometh out of the wilderness like pillars of smoke?"* (Song 3:6), but then their attention was claimed by the pomp and state of the King, not by His person or by that of His bride. Here, on the other hand, they are attracted by the happy position of the bride in relation to her Beloved, and not by their surroundings. *"Who is this that cometh up from the wilderness, leaning upon her beloved?"* (Song 8:5).

It is through the bride that attention is drawn to the Bridegroom. Their union and communion are now open and manifest. For the last time, the wilderness is mentioned, but sweetly solaced by the presence of the Bridegroom, it is not a wilderness to this bride. In all the trustfulness of confiding love she is seen leaning upon her Beloved. He is her strength, her joy, her pride, and her prize, while she is His special treasure, the object of His tenderest care. All His resources of wisdom and might are hers. She is at rest, though journeying; she is satisfied, though in the wilderness, all the while leaning upon her Beloved.

However wonderful the revelations of grace and love to the heart are, which are taught by the Holy Spirit through the relationship of bride and Bridegroom, the Christ of God is more than a Bridegroom to His people. He who was able to say, when on earth, *"Before Abraham was, I am"* (John 8:58), here claims His bride from her very birth and not only from the time of her betrothal. Before she knew Him, He knew her, and He reminds her of this in the following words: *"I raised thee up under the apple tree: there thy mother brought thee forth"* (Song 8:5).

He takes delight in her beauty, but that is not so much the cause as the effect of His love, for He took her up when she had no beauty. The Love that has made her what she is, and now takes delight in her, is not a fickle love; she does not need to fear its change.

The bride gladly recognizes this truth, that she is indeed His own, and she exclaims,

> *Set me as a seal upon thine heart, as a*
> *seal upon thine arm: for love is strong as*
> *death; jealousy* [ardent love] *is cruel*
> [certain] *as the grave: the coals thereof*
> *are coals of fire, which hath a most ve-*
> *hement flame.* (Song 8:6)

Israel's high priest bore the names of the twelve tribes upon his heart. Each name was engraved as a seal in the costly and imperishable stone chosen by God. Each seal or stone was set in the purest gold. The priest likewise bore the same names upon his shoulders, indicating that both the love and the strength of the high priest were pledged on behalf of the tribes of Israel. In this same way, the bride desires to be sustained by Him who is alike her Prophet, Priest, and King, for love is as strong as death and ardent love as certain as the grave. Not that she doubts the constancy of her Beloved, but she has learned the inconstancy of her own heart. She wants to be bound to the heart and arm of her Beloved as with chains and settings of gold, which are always the emblem of divinity. As the psalmist prayed, *"Bind the sacrifice with cords, even unto the horns of the altar"* (Ps. 118:27).

It is comparatively easy to lay the sacrifice on the altar that sanctifies the gift, but it

requires divine compulsion—the cords of love—
to leave it there. So here the bride desires to be
set and fixed on the heart and on the arm of
Him who is from this time on to be her all in all,
so that she may always trust only in that love
and be sustained only by that power.

Do we not need to learn a lesson from this
and to pray to be kept from turning to Egypt for
help, from trusting in horses and chariots (Isa.
31:1), from putting confidence in princes or in
man, rather than in the living God (Ps. 118:8–
9)? How the kings of Israel, who had won great
triumphs by faith, sometimes turned aside to
heathen nations in their later years! May the
Lord keep His people from this snare.

UNQUENCHABLE LOVE

The Bridegroom replies to the bride's re-
quest with reassuring words:

> *Many waters cannot quench love, neither
> can the floods drown it: if a man would
> give all the substance of his house for
> love, it would utterly be contemned.*
>
> *(Song 8:7)*

The love that grace has begotten in the
heart of the bride is itself divine and persistent.
Many waters cannot quench it, and the floods

cannot drown it. Suffering and pain, bereavement and loss, may test its constancy, but they will not quench it. Its source is not human or natural. Like the fire (Song 8:6), it is hidden with Christ in God.

> [What] *shall separate us from the love of Christ? shall tribulation, or distress, or persecution, or famine, or nakedness, or peril, or sword?...Nay, in all these things we are more than conquerors through him that loved us. For I am persuaded, that neither death, nor life, nor angels, nor principalities, nor powers, nor things present, nor things to come, nor height, nor depth, nor any other* [creation, RV margin], *shall be able to separate us from the love of God, which is in Christ Jesus our Lord.*   (Rom. 8:35, 37–39)

Our love for God is secured by God's love for us. To the soul really rescued by grace, no bribe to forsake God's love will be fully successful. *"If a man would give all the substance of his house for love, it would utterly be contemned"* (Song 8:7).

FELLOWSHIP WITH THE BRIDEGROOM

Freed from anxiety on her own account, the happy bride next asks for guidance and

fellowship in service with her Lord on behalf of
those who have not yet reached her favored
position. *"We have a little sister, and she hath
no breasts: what shall we do for our sister in
the day when she shall be spoken for?"* (Song
8:8).

How beautifully her conscious union with
the Bridegroom appears in her expressions. *"We
have a little sister,"* not *I* have. *"What shall we
do for our sister?"* She now has no private rela-
tionships or interests. In all things she is one
with Him. And we see a further development of
grace in the very question. Toward the close of
the last section, she recognized the Bridegroom
as her Instructor. She will not now make her
own plans about her little sister and ask His ac-
quiescence in them. Instead, she will learn what
His thoughts are and have fellowship with Him
in His plans.

How much anxiety and care the children
of God would be spared if they learned to act in
this way! Is it not quite common to make the
best plans that we can and to carry them out
as best we may, all the while feeling a great
burden of responsibility and earnestly asking
the Lord to help us? However, if we would always let Him be our Instructor and leave the
responsibility with Him, our strength would
not be exhausted with worry and anxiety, but

would all be at His disposal and would accomplish His ends.

In the little sister, still immature, we see the elect of God, given to Christ in God's purpose, but not yet brought into saving relation to Him. And perhaps we may also see those babes in Christ who still need feeding with milk and not with meat, but who, with such care, will in due time become experienced believers, fitted for the service of the Lord. Then they will be spoken for and called into that department of service for which He has prepared them.

The Bridegroom replies, *"If she be a wall, we will build upon her a palace of silver: and if she be a door, we will enclose her with boards of cedar"* (Song 8:9). In this reply the Bridegroom sweetly recognizes His oneness with His bride in the same way that she has shown her conscious oneness with Him. When she says, *"What shall we do for our sister?"* He replies, *"We will build...we will enclose."* He will not carry out His purposes of grace irrespective of His bride, but He will work with and through her. What can be done for this sister, however, will depend upon what she becomes. If she is a wall, built upon the true foundation, strong and stable, she will be adorned and beautified with battlements of silver. But, if she is unstable and easily moved, like a door, such treatment will be as impossible as it is unsuitable. She will need to be enclosed with boards of cedar, hedged in with restraints for her own protection.

The bride responds rejoicingly, *"I am a wall"* (Song 8:10). She knows the foundation on which she is built. There is no "if" in her case. She is conscious of having found favor in the eyes of her Beloved. Naphtali's blessing is hers; she is *"satisfied with favour, and full with the blessing of the LORD"* (Deut. 33:23).

But what do the lines that follow teach in connection with this happy consciousness?

Solomon had a vineyard at Baalhamon; he let out the vineyard unto keepers; every one for the fruit thereof was to bring a thousand pieces of silver. My vineyard, which is mine, is before me: thou, O Solomon, must have a thousand, and those that keep the fruit thereof two hundred. (Song 8:11–12)

The connection is, I believe, one of great importance, teaching us that what she *was,* by grace, was more important than what she *did.* It is also important to note that she did not work in order to earn favor but, being assured of favor, gave her love free range to show itself in service. The bride knew her relationship to her Lord and His love for her, and in her determination that He should have the thousand pieces of silver, her concern was that her vineyard should not produce less for her Solomon than His vineyard at Baalhamon. Her vineyard was herself, and she desired much fruit for her Lord. She would see, too, that the keepers of the vineyard, those who were her companions in its cultivation, and who ministered in word and doctrine, were well rewarded. She would not muzzle the ox that treads out the corn (Deut. 25:4); a full tithe, no, more than that, a double tithe, was to be the portion of those who kept the fruit and labored with her in the vineyard.

GLORIFIED TOGETHER!

How long this happy service continues, and how soon it is to be terminated, we cannot tell. He who calls His servants to dwell in the gardens and cultivate them for Him—as Adam of old was placed in the Paradise of God—is the only One who knows the limit of this service. Sooner or later, eternal rest will come: the burden and heat of the Last Day will have been endured, the last conflict will be over, and the voice of the Bridegroom will be heard addressing His loved one, *"Thou that dwellest in*

*the gardens, the companions hearken to thy
voice: cause me to hear it"* (Song 8:13).

The Bridegroom is saying, "Your service
among the companions is finished. You have
fought the good fight. You have kept the faith,
and you have finished your course (2 Tim. 4:7).
From this time forward, there is laid up for
you the crown of righteousness (v. 8)." The
Bridegroom Himself will be your exceedingly
great reward!

The bride may well let Him hear her voice,
and, springing forth in heart to meet Him, cry,
*"Make haste, my beloved, and be thou like to a
roe or to a young hart upon the mountains of
spices"* (Song 8:14). She no longer asks Him, as
in the second section, *"Turn, my beloved, and
be thou like a roe or a young hart upon the
mountains of Bether* [separation]*"* (Song 2:17).

Since that time, she has never again
wished Him to turn away from her, for there
are no mountains of Bether to those who are
abiding in Christ; now there are mountains of
spices. He who inhabits the praises of Israel,
which rise like the incense of spices from His
people's hearts, is invited by His bride to make
haste, to come quickly and be like a roe or
young hart upon the mountains of spices.

The presence of our Lord is very sweet,
since by His Spirit He dwells among His people

while they serve Him below. But here there
are many thorns in every path, which call for
watchful care, and it is proper that now we
should suffer with our Lord so that we may
hereafter be glorified together. The day, however, is soon coming in which He will bring us
up out of the earthly gardens and associations
to the palace of the great King. There His people

> *shall hunger no more, neither thirst any*
> *more; neither shall the sun light on*
> *them, nor any heat. For the Lamb which*
> *is in the midst of the throne shall feed*
> *them, and shall lead them unto living*
> *fountains of waters: and God shall wipe*
> *away all tears from their eyes.*
>
> *(Rev. 7:16–17)*

> *The Spirit and the bride say, Come....*
> *Surely I come quickly. Amen. Even so,*
> *come, Lord Jesus.*
>
> *(Rev. 22:17, 20)*

Chapter 8

The Daughters of Jerusalem

The question is frequently asked, Who are represented by the daughters of Jerusalem? They are clearly not the bride, yet they are not far removed from her.

They know where the Bridegroom makes His flock to rest at noon. They are charged by the Bridegroom not to stir up or awaken His love when she rests, abiding in Him. They draw attention to the Bridegroom when He comes up from the wilderness with dignity and pomp. Their love gifts adorn His chariot of state. They are appealed to by the bride for help in finding her Beloved, and, stirred by her impassioned description of His beauty, they desire to seek Him with her.

They describe the beauty of the bride quite fully, but, on the other hand, they never seem to be occupied with the person of the Bridegroom. He is not all in all to them; they only seem to care for outward and earthly things.

Could they possibly represent those who, if not actually saved, are very near it, or, if saved, are not fully committed? Could they be those who are for the present more concerned about the things of this world than the things of God? To advance their own interests, to secure their own comfort, concerns them more than to be pleasing to the Lord in all things.

They may form part of that great company, spoken of in Revelation 7:9–17, that comes out of the Great Tribulation, but they will not form part of the 144,000, *"the firstfruits unto God and to the Lamb"* (Rev. 14:4). They have forgotten the warning of our Lord in Luke 21:34–36, and hence they are not *"accounted worthy to escape all these things that shall come to pass, and to stand before the Son of man"* (v. 36). They have not, with Paul, counted *"all things but loss for the excellency of the knowledge of Christ Jesus"* (Phil. 3:8), and hence they do not *"attain unto the resurrection of the dead"* (Phil. 3:11), which Paul felt he might miss but aimed to attain to.

I wish to place on record my solemn conviction that not all who are Christians or think themselves to be such, will attain to that resurrection of which Paul speaks in Philippians 3:11, or will *"meet the Lord in the air"* (1 Thess. 4:17). To those who show by lives of consecration that they are not of the world, but are looking for Him, *"shall he appear...without sin unto salvation"* (Heb. 9:28).